GW01607950
£1·00

SBN 361 03893 3

Published 1977 by Purnell Books, Berkshire House, Queen Street, Maidenhead, Berkshire
Made and printed in Great Britain by Purnell and Sons Limited, Paulton (Avon) and London

BIG NODDY BOOK

By

Enid Blyton

LONDON
SAMPSON LOW, MARSTON & CO. LTD.
AND DENNIS DOBSON, LTD.

CONTENTS

ONE day, when Noddy was driving his little car along the road, he saw the Toyland Train in the distance. It seemed to be going along very slowly indeed.

"I wonder what's wrong with it!" said Noddy. "I'll soon see, because the road runs alongside the railway in a minute. Goodness—I must be going faster than the train!"

He soon caught up with the train—and then he saw why it was going so very slowly! It was passing some blackberry hedges—and will you believe it, the engine-driver was leaning out, picking big ripe blackberries as he passed the hedges!

"Well—no wonder it's a *slow* train today!" thought Noddy. "I'll race past it, and then perhaps the driver will be ashamed and drive properly."

As he was racing by, something dreadful happened! The engine-driver leaned out too far to pick an extra big blackberry—and fell right out of the cab of his engine!

So the train went on without him! He got up and ran after

it. "Wait for me, train! You can't drive yourself! Oh, there'll be an accident!"

Then he saw Noddy in his little car. "Oh, Noddy—*you*

must save the train and all the people in it! Drive after it—catch it up—leap out of your little car and jump into my engine-cab. It's quite easy to drive the train."

"Good *gracious*!" said Noddy. "Me drive the Toyland Train? Oh, I've wanted to do that for ages and ages!"

He didn't even stop to pick up the worried engine-driver, but drove straight on at top speed. He was soon just a little in front of the slow, puffing engine. He jumped out of his car and ran to it. With a mighty leap he was on the step of the engine-cab—and there he was, in the engine-driver's place!

His heart beat fast. Soon a corner was coming and he

must guide the engine safely round it. Then there was a bridge—he really must be careful when the train puffed over that! And what about that dark tunnel?

Noddy looked at all the handles and knobs. Perhaps it would be best to find the one that stopped the train? Was it this one?

"Oh no—that makes it go *faster*!" said Noddy. "Well, perhaps it's this one. Goodness, that makes it whistle! Oh dear—I hope I'm going to be a *good* engine-driver! Now—I must try hard."

Well, of course, Noddy knew exactly how to drive a car—and it didn't take him very long to find out how to drive a train. Soon he had found out what all the knobs and handles were for, and drove the train along beautifully.

He was very excited. Whoever would think he could

drive the Toyland Train so well? Soon he would arrive at Toyland Village Station, and *how* surprised everyone would be to see *him* driving the train!

"Oh, I hope Big-Ears will be there—and perhaps little Tessie Bear. I do so want them to see me driving the train!" thought Noddy. "Ah—here's the bridge. Careful now!"

The train went over the bridge safely, and then came the long dark tunnel. Noddy didn't like that very much, but they

soon came out into the daylight again—and there, in the distance, was Toyland Station! Noddy pulled the knob that made the engine whistle.

"Pheeeeeeee! Pheeeeeeee!" The whistle was very loud, and the train puffed proudly into the station, chuffity-chuff, chuffity-chuff! Noddy looked out of the engine-cab—and there was Big-Ears on the platform!

"Noddy! Noddy, whatever *are* you doing?" cried

Big-Ears. " Goodness me, Noddy—surely you're not driving the train ! Mr. Plod, look who's driving the train ! Tessie Bear, Miss Fluffy Cat, look all of you—Noddy's driving the Toyland Train ! Whatever next ! "

Mr. Plod wouldn't let him drive it any further—but oh what a fuss everyone made of him. He really was quite a hero—and do you know what he told Tessie Bear ?

" I'm going to save up to buy a train for myself ! " he said. " And then I'll drive you all over the place, Tessie ! "

Dear little Noddy—I'm afraid you'll never have enough money for that !

"NODDY! Please will you go and fetch me one dozen eggs from the farm," said Big-Ears, when he called one morning at Noddy's little house. "My brother Little-Ears is coming to dinner, and bringing a friend."

"Oh yes, Big-Ears. Of course I'll get the eggs for you," said Noddy. "I'll run up to the farm in my little car."

"If I'm not in when you bring them to my Toadstool House, pop them into my larder, please," said Big-Ears, getting on his bicycle and riding off again. "Sorry I can't wait. Just going to get a new loaf of bread and some butter."

Noddy was so afraid that he might forget to fetch the eggs that he wrote out a little note and put it into the driving seat of his car. He finished cleaning the car, and then fetched a basket and got into the driving seat.

"Ah—there's my note, with EGGS written on it," he said. "I'll go straight to the farm before I forget. Big-Ears doesn't like it when I don't do what he asks me to."

Away he went in his little car. Parp-parp! It hooted at pretty Angela Golden-Hair. Parp-parp! It hooted at Bruiny Bear. Parp-parp! It even hooted at Mr. Plod!

"Ah—there goes little Noddy," said everyone. "We

always know when *he's* about!"

Noddy soon came to the farm. Mrs. Straw was very busy making lovely yellow pats of butter in her little dairy.

"Hello, little Noddy," she said. "What do you want?"

"Twelve nice new-laid eggs, please," said Noddy. "Oooh, can I taste that butter?"

"No, keep your fingers out of it," said Mrs. Straw. "See how dirty your hands are! Dear, dear—I don't believe you washed them this morning."

"I did," said Noddy. "But I got them dirty again cleaning the car. Where are the eggs, Mrs. Straw?"

"Well, there now—I've sent them all off to the market," said Mrs. Straw. "But you can go and look in the nests, Noddy—I expect the hens will have laid some more. You can take a dozen."

So Noddy took his basket, and went to look for eggs in

the nests. He went into the hen-houses, but not one single egg was in any of the nests.

He met a hen and spoke to it. "Hen—do you know where there are any eggs?"

"Cluck-cluck!" said the hen and scuttled away.

Then Noddy saw a hen sitting in a little wooden coop, on a nice big nest. "Hallo, hen," he said. "Have you any eggs there?"

"Cluck-cluck!" said the hen proudly, and got off her nest to show him a beautiful batch of white eggs.

"Oh, they're lovely!" said Noddy, and counted them. "Yes—you've twelve eggs. Just what I want!" And he picked them up one by one and put them into his basket.

"Cluck-cluck!" said the hen, angrily, and gave him a sudden peck on his hand.

"Oooh, don't," said Noddy. "That's unkind. There—that's all the eggs. I'd better take some of this soft hay too, in case they joggle about and break when they are in my car."

Soon he was back in his car again, the basket of eggs beside him. What nice big eggs! Big-Ears would be very, very pleased!

Noddy drove carefully back to the toadstool house. He

stopped, got out, and took the basket of eggs. He went up to the door and called loudly.

"Big-Ears! Are you back yet? I've brought the eggs."

There was no answer, so Noddy opened the door and went inside. The cat was there, dozing by the fire. "Hallo, cat," said Noddy. "I've brought the eggs for Big-Ears. I'm going to put them into the larder."

He opened the larder door and carefully put the eggs one by one into a dish, with the soft hay under them. Then he shut the door and went out. The cat didn't even look at him.

Now not long after Noddy had gone, the cat pricked up its ears. It could hear a strange noise somewhere. Yes—from the larder! Whatever could it be? It got up and strolled over to the door. Then it grew very excited and began to miaow, and to scratch at the door.

It was still doing this when Big-Ears came in with Little-Ears, and his friend, Mr. Whiskers Rabbit.

"Goodness—what's the matter with your cat?" said Little-Ears to his brother. "Is your larder full of fish or something?"

"No. What's the matter, puss? Why are you so excited?" said Big-Ears, going to the larder-door. "Get away from my feet."

Big-Ears opened the larder-door—and then he stared in amazement! The larder shelves were full of tiny yellow chicks! The cat nearly went mad, and Little-Ears only just caught hold of it in time, or it would have leapt on the shelves to catch the chicks.

"Look at that!" said Big-Ears, as the tiny chicks scrambled about over his pies and tarts and sausage rolls. "Wherever did they come from? Oh dear—I suppose it is a silly joke of Noddy's. I asked him to bring me some eggs—and he brought me chicks instead. Really, he's very foolish sometimes!"

Big-Ears caught all the tiny chicks and put them into a box so that the cat could not get them. He felt very cross

with Noddy. What a thing to do! Well, he would certainly scold him about it when he came along that afternoon.

He set out a nice meal for Little-Ears and Mr. Whiskers Rabbit. "I'm very sorry there are no eggs," he said. "And I don't expect anyone wants to gobble up one of those dear little chicks! Really—what a surprising thing to find in my larder!"

Just before tea there came a rap at Big-Ears' door. It was Noddy, hoping to be asked to tea. But Big-Ears was not smiling when he opened the door.

"Noddy," he said, in a stern voice, "I'm not pleased with you. Why did you bring me twelve chicks instead of twelve new-laid eggs?"

"I didn't," said Noddy, in surprise. "I went to choose the eggs myself at Farmer Straw's. Mrs. Straw said I could take any I found in the nests."

"Well, dear me—*where* did

the chicks come from then ?" said Big-Ears, astonished. "Look, Noddy—they're in this box—the dearest little fluffy things ! Who could have brought them ? And where are the *eggs* you said you brought ?"

Then suddenly Little-Ears began to laugh. He laughed and laughed, and Big-Ears stared at him in surprise.

"Oh Big-Ears—haven't you guessed what has happened ?" said Little-Ears, chuckling. "Silly little Noddy here went to take eggs from a hen who was hatching some out ! Not new-laid eggs at all ! And he brought them here, and put the eggs into your dish, with that hay we saw. . . ."

"Good gracious—and they all hatched out in my larder !" cried Big-Ears. "No wonder my old cat was so excited when she heard them cheeping there ! I suppose the eggshells are in that dish. Well—what a thing to happen !"

"Oh dear !" said Noddy, in alarm. "What *will* Mrs. Straw say ? Will she be very cross with me ? What shall I do ?"

"Put that box into your car and take back all the chicks," said Big-Ears. "Really, Noddy—fancy taking the eggs from under a sitting hen ! Wasn't she cross ?"

"Yes—she pecked me, look," said Noddy. "Oh dear—

I'm always getting into trouble. The hen will be angry with me, and so will Mrs. Straw."

"Well, it's your own fault," said Big-Ears. "You knew chicks came out of eggs, didn't you? So do ducklings—and sometimes little snakes come out of *snake*-eggs!"

"Good *gracious*!" said Noddy. "I'll never have an egg for my breakfast again! I just *won't* have a snake gliding about my breakfast table!"

"Now you take these chicks back to Mrs. Straw and let her give them to the mother-hen," said Big-Ears, "And then come back here and have tea with us. Well, well, well—I simply *never* know what you're going to do next!"

Noddy really is funny, isn't he? I do hope the mother-hen won't peck him again!

BIG-EARS' CAT GETS INTO TROUBLE

One morning Noddy was on his way to see Big-Ears, when he saw someone waving to him from the pavement. " Oh—it's little Tessie Bear ! " he thought. " Good ! I'll take her for a ride in my car. Hey, Tessie—jump in ! "

Tessie was very pleased. " I hope you aren't very busy, Noddy," she said. " Have you many jobs to do ? "

" No, I was going to see Big-Ears," said Noddy, and away they went at top speed through the wood.

Big-Ears was very pleased to see little Tessie Bear. He shook hands with her, and said he liked the bow under her chin.

" Noddy—where's my shopping ? " he said. " And did you remember to bring back my umbrella that I lent you ? "

" Oh *dear* ! " said Noddy, and took an empty basket from his car. " I *meant* to fetch your shopping, Big-Ears. And I *meant* to bring your umbrella. I'm very sorry ! " But Big-Ears was cross, and wouldn't ask Noddy into his house.

" I'd got cakes and lemonade ready for you, but you don't deserve any now," he said. " Please go away."

So Noddy drove sadly away with Tessie Bear and the empty basket. " Nasty old Big-Ears ! " said Noddy.

" He *was* cross," said Tessie. " Oh, Noddy—what's that loud noise in the wood ? Stop a minute, please."

So they stopped—and Tessie soon found out what was making the noise. " Look," she said, " there's a cat . . . .

" Right at the top of that tree. It can't get down, poor thing." Noddy looked. "Gracious!" he said. "It's Big-Ears' cat!"

" Well—he was so horrid to me just now that I won't bother about his silly cat." And he got back into the car.

Little Tessie Bear was shocked. " Oh *Noddy* ! The poor frightened cat ! Well —I'm going to stay and try to help it."

" I'll stay too," said Noddy. " I didn't *mean* what I said. I like Big-Ears' cat. I'll climb up and get it. Here goes . . . ."

Noddy climbed right up to the very top of the tree—but although the cat miaowed loudly, it wouldn't go down.

" It's afraid," called down Noddy. " What can we do, Tessie ? " " I'll throw up the basket," said Tessie. . . . .

" Then you can put the cat into it and climb down." So she threw up the basket, and Noddy put the cat into it.

But oh dear—he couldn't climb down with the heavy cat in the basket, because he needed both hands to climb with !

He nearly fell down himself. Whatever was he to do ? Then he scrambled down the tree quickly. . . .

" I've a good idea, Tessie," he said. " I've left the cat safely up there in the basket, look, but what we want is. . . .

" Some rope or something to tie to it so that I can gently let the basket down to the ground. Now, let's think." " Let's tie your shoe-laces together—and your scarf—and my belt ! " said Tessie. " They will make a fine rope."

BIG-EARS' CAT GETS INTO TROUBLE

So Noddy untied his shoe laces and took off his scarf, and Tessie gave him her belt, and now see. . . .

They are all tied together into a fine rope ! Up to the tree goes Noddy again, and now he ties the queer rope. . . .

To the handle of the basket. The cat miaowed. "It's all right," said Noddy. "I'm going to let you down the tree. . . .

"Like this—very gently. Don't bump against the branches. Hold tight, cat. Tessie, it's coming down, be ready !"

The basket swung slowly down the tree on the strange rope. Now Tessie is reaching out her arms for it.

And she caught the basket safely in her arms ! The cat jumped down, mewing loudly. It was very pleased.

And then who should come up but Big-Ears! How surprised he was to see what Tessie and Noddy were doing!

"Your cat was up the tree and couldn't get down," said Tessie. "So we made a rope and Noddy climbed up."

"You're very very kind—especially as I was cross with you," said Big-Ears, picking up his cat. "You're to come back with me this very minute, and have those cakes and lemonade. Come along!"

So they all went back to Big-Ears' house in the car, though it was a bit of a squash because the cat came too.

And now what a feast they are having. You can hardly see Noddy because the cat *will* sit on his knee!

See how well you can paint or crayon this picture of Mrs. Tubby's tea-party.

NODDY HAS A FUNNY IDEA

ONE day when Noddy drove up to the Toadstool House to call on his friend Big-Ears, he had a great surprise Big-Ears was packing his suit-case to go away !

" Oh Big-Ears ! " said Noddy, " you didn't tell me you were going away ! Where are you going ? "

" My brother Little-Ears wants me," said Big-Ears. " He's going to paint his house and I said I would go and help him."

" I'll come too," said Noddy. " I'd like to paint a house —splish-splash-splish-splash ! "

" I daresay you would," said Big-Ears. " But Little-Ears doesn't want you, Noddy. Don't you remember—last time you went there, he asked you to weed his garden—and you pulled up all his seedlings."

" Well—they *looked* like weeds," said Noddy. " All right. I won't come. But I shall miss you, Big-Ears. Are you going to take your cat with you ? "

" No, I can't," said Big-Ears. " The smell of new paint makes him sick. I wondered if Mr. Plod would look after him for me."

" Mr. Plod ! But he doesn't *like* cats," said Noddy.

"No—*I'll* look after your old cat for you, Big-Ears."

"He'd never stay with you!" said Big-Ears. "He hardly ever *looks* at you."

"He *is* rather a stand-offish cat," said Noddy, nodding his head. "But I know how to keep him close to me ALL the time, Big-Ears."

"You don't," said Big-Ears. "He won't come near you! And he'd run away from your house as soon as you took him there."

"He wouldn't," said Noddy. "I'll just show you. Wait here a minute, Big-Ears."

Noddy ran out to his little car. He had his shopping there, and in one parcel was some fish for his dinner. Noddy did a MOST peculiar thing with it! He unwrapped it from its paper, put the fish down on the grass—and wiped his feet on it! Yes—he really did. He wiped them and wiped them. Then he cut the piece of fish in half—and put a piece into each of his pockets!

Then he went back to Big-Ears' house. "Puss, Puss, Puss!" he called.

To Big-Ears' enormous surprise the cat ran round Noddy, purring loudly, and rubbed its head against Noddy's feet.

" Now—you come with me, cat," said Noddy. " Keep close to me and don't run away. Come along ! "

And the cat kept close to Noddy and went purring with him to the car ! Big-Ears went to the gate in astonishment.

" Noddy ! Why does my cat suddenly follow you like that ? " he called. " Is it a spell ? "

" Well—a *kind* of spell ! " shouted back Noddy, as the cat settled comfortably beside him in his car. " Have a good time, Big-Ears. I promise you that your cat will never leave me as long as you are away ! "

Well, well ! Big-Ears was really very, very puzzled. His old cat had NEVER behaved with anyone in such a way before. Certainly not with Noddy ! He finished his packing, got on his bicycle, and rode off to Little-Ears' house, still feeling surprised.

Mr. and Mrs. Tubby Bear were surprised too, when they saw how Big-Ears' cat followed Noddy about everywhere. " Why he might be *your* cat," said Mrs. Tubby. " He never leaves you, Noddy ! He's always rubbing against your legs and purring. He must be very, very fond of you ! "

Big-Ears came back in two days time and went to Noddy's house to collect his cat. " I wonder if my old cat is still purring round Noddy," he thought. " I'm sure he's not ! He's either run away back to my house—or Noddy has had to keep him shut up somewhere."

Noddy was outside, cleaning his car. Big-Ears saw him there—and saw the cat too. Goodness gracious—it was actually lying down on Noddy's feet ! When Noddy moved, the cat jumped off, followed him round, rubbing its head against him and purring all the time. Big-Ears couldn't understand it. Why, his cat had never loved *him* like that !

" Hey, Noddy ! " he called. " I'm back—and I see my cat is still loving you. What is this wonderful cat-spell you've got ? Do tell me ! "

" Well, if you like, I'll get a bit of the spell and rub it

on *you* ! " said Noddy, with a laugh. " Wait there, Big-Ears."

He hurried indoors and fetched a bit of fish. " Shut your eyes ! " he called as he came out with it—and then he rubbed it over Big-Ears' shoes.

" Now walk out of the gate and your cat will come at once ! " he said. And, of course, as soon as Big-Ears walked away, the cat, smelling the fresh fish, ran after him at once.

" Wonderful ! " said Big-Ears. " I'll buy the secret of that spell from you Noddy. Look—here's a shilling for it ! "

" All right ! " said Noddy. " I just rubbed some fish on your boots. Ha ha ! That's all it was—and you gave me a shilling for that ! Let's go and spend it at the ice-cream shop—but first I'll change my shoes. I'm getting a bit tired of smelling fishy all the time ! "

Well—what an idea ! No wonder Big-Ears' cat wouldn't leave Noddy for a single minute !

NODDY'S EXCITING RIDE

A game for two or more players

Noddy went off for a quiet ride in his car one day when he started to have the most amazing adventures before he reached his House-for-One. Play this game and follow Noddy's adventures in his car.

Ask Mummy for a different coloured counter or button for each player and a dice in an egg-cup. You then take turns to throw, but you must get a six to start.

SLEEPING
MISS TURN
DANGEROUS CURVE
GO BACK TO 30
HAVING TEA
WITH BIG EARS
MISS 2 TURNS
BRIDGE, FOR-
WARD TO 54
GOLLY
GARAGE
GARAGE,
FORWARD
TO 70
ICE-CREAM
FOR DOLL
BACK TO 71
24 25 26 27 28 29 30 31 32 33 34 35 36 37 38 39 40 41 42 43 44 45 46 47 48 49 50 51 52 53 54 55 56 57 58 59 60 61 62 63 64 65 66
73 74 75 76 77 78 79 80

BIG-EARS' UMBRELLA

NOW one day Noddy took little Tessie Bear to have tea with Big-Ears, because Big-Ears was very fond of her. When it was time to take her home again, it was raining.

"It's *pouring*!" said Noddy in dismay. "Oh, Tessie, you'll get so wet in my car. I *wish* I'd brought my umbrella. Big-Ears, will you lend me yours?"

"No," said Big-Ears. "Every time I lend it to you, you forget to bring it back. I told you I wouldn't lend it to you any more, and I meant it."

"But Big-Ears—it's for little Tessie Bear," said Noddy. "Her new hat will be spoilt. She'll get a cold. She will shiver and shake and . . ."

"All right, all right, I'll lend it to you," said Big-Ears. "But *really* I'm lending it to Tessie. And you're to bring it back *tomorrow*, Noddy. If you don't I shall take the bell off your cap and sew it on mine—just to teach you that I mean what I say."

"Oh thank you, Big-Ears, you *are* kind to lend us your umbrella," said Noddy and ran to the corner where it stood.

" It's such a lovely big one, it will cover us both. *You* can hold it while I drive, Tessie, can't you ? "

" Oh yes," said Tessie. " What a beauty, isn't it—so big—and what a lovely colour ! "

Soon they were out in the little car and Noddy put up the big umbrella. It sheltered both of them from the pouring rain. " Now you hold the handle, Tessie," said Noddy. " And I'll drive."

Away they went, quite slowly, the big umbrella over them. Mr. Jumbo and Mr. Wobbly-Man laughed to see them, as they passed by them in Toy Village.

Noddy took Tessie safely home—and by that time the rain had stopped, so they could close the umbrella. " Goodbye, Noddy," said Tessie. " I had a lovely time—and please, Noddy—you *will* remember to take back the umbrella to Big-Ears tomorrow, won't you ? Promise ? "

"I promise," said Noddy, and away he went, the umbrella beside him on the seat. He took it indoors with him when he got home, determined not to forget it next day. He stood it beside him while he had his supper.

"I'm not going to let you out of my sight!" he said. "You stand there, umbrella—and when I go to bed, you're going to go too, so that nobody can steal you in the night!"

It was funny to see the umbrella lying beside Noddy in bed, its handle sticking out from under the clothes like a head. Noddy found it rather uncomfortable when he turned over in the middle of the night. "What's this?" he said. "Oh its you, umbrella. Move up a bit. You're dreadfully hard and long."

Noddy stood it beside his breakfast table next morning, and he took it to the garage with him when he went to clean his car. He stood it close beside him so that he should keep seeing it. That would remind him that he MUST keep his promise and take it back to Big-Ears.

At last his car was shining and clean. Noddy washed his hands and got into the driving seat. He put the umbrella beside him in the passenger's seat, and there it was, trying to look like a proper passenger!

"Now we'll go to Big-Ears," said Noddy. "And NOTHING will stop me from delivering you safely, umbrella. You'll soon be standing in your own little corner of Toadstool House."

But something did stop him! Halfway through the village who should come galloping across the road in front of the car but Bumpy, the toy dog! Noddy put on his brakes and just stopped in time.

"You silly dog Bumpy!" he shouted, crossly. "What do you mean by prancing about in front of my car like that? I might have run you over!"

"Wuffy-wuff!" said Bumpy joyfully, and ran up to Noddy and gave him an enormous lick on his nose.

"DON'T!" said Noddy. "Why are you so licky? *I* don't go round licking everyone!"

"Wuff!" said Bumpy, and leapt into the seat beside Noddy. Noddy pushed him out at once.

"NO!" he said. "Can't you see I've got Big-Ears' umbrella there? I'm taking it back to him because he lent it to me—and I *promised* he should have it today. I'm not taking anyone in my car till he's got it back."

Bumpy jumped into the car again—and oh dear, Noddy

gave him such a smack that he jumped out at once, put his tail down and looked very miserable indeed. " Wuff ! " he said, in a very, very small voice.

Noddy started off again—and then he stopped. Something was wrong with one of his tyres—what was it ? He jumped out to see.

" Oh ! " I've got a big stone stuck in my back tyre ! " he said. " I must get it out before it makes a hole. But oh dear—what shall I get it out with ? Oh—*I* know—I'll poke it out with Big-Ears' umbrella ! Just the thing ! "

So he got Big-Ears' umbrella and poked out the big stone. Bumpy came to watch, his tail down. But Noddy was still cross with him.

" Go away ! You're a nuisance. If you lick my nose again you'll get another smack, Bumpy Dog ! " Then he got into his car and drove away at top speed. Aha ! That was the way to treat the Bumpy Dog if he made a nuisance of himself !

The Bumpy Dog sat down sorrowfully on the pavement. He did like Noddy so much and he couldn't *bear* being

smacked. Then he suddenly saw something lying on the pavement.

Will you believe it, it was Big-Ears' umbrella! Yes—Noddy had forgotten to put it back into his car again. He had driven off without it. The Bumpy Dog looked and looked at it. What had Noddy said? He had said he was taking it back to Big-Ears—and now he had forgotten it!

Bumpy made up his mind at once. He would race after Noddy with it, and give it to him. Then perhaps he wouldn't be cross with him any more. So away he trotted, with the big umbrella in his mouth.

Noddy was a long way ahead. He had reached Big-Ears' house and Big-Ears came to meet him. "Well, Noddy—so you've come to give me back my umbrella?" he said, pleased.

"Yes," said Noddy, and looked for it on the seat beside him. But it wasn't there!

"Oh! I left it behind on the pavement in Toy Village!" he said. "Goodness me, someone may have taken it by now! Oh Big-Ears, I did mean to bring it. I'll go straight back and . . ."

"There! You've forgotten it *again*!" said Big-Ears, really cross—and oh dear, he took a pair of scissors from his

pocket and snipped off the bell on the top of Noddy's hat! "Now it's *my* bell—and I shall sew it on *my* hat!"

Noddy began to wail. "No, no—I tell you I was *bringing* your umbrella here, I really was, Big-Ears. Please let me have my bell. Big-Ears, I tell you. . . ."

But Big-Ears had gone into his house to sew the bell on *his* hat. Oh dear! But wait a minute, who was this panting up the woodland path?

"It's Bumpy!" cried Noddy. "And oh, he's got the umbrella! You saw I'd left it behind, Bumpy—and though I'd smacked you and been cross, you still wanted to help me. Bumpy, I love you, I think you're very, very kind."

And he jumped out of his car, and ran to hug Bumpy very hard indeed. Bumpy was so pleased. Then Noddy went to give Big-Ears the umbrella.

"Here it is—you're *not* to sew my bell on your hat!" he cried, and he took away his little bell at once. Big-Ears laughed.

"All right. I don't know how you managed to find my umbrella so quickly—but you're only just in time to have back your bell. Shall I sew it on your hat for you?"

"No. I'm lending it to someone else for the day," said Noddy. And what do you suppose he did? He let the Bumpy Dog sit beside him in the car, and he drove to the market and bought a blue ribbon for him. Then he threaded the bell on to the ribbon and hung it round Bumpy's neck. It went jingle-jingle-jing all the time.

Bumpy was so proud and pleased that he really didn't know what to do! He galloped and pranced and bounded and skipped till Noddy felt quite dizzy.

"Bring it back tomorrow," he said to Bumpy. "But now you can go and show it to little Tessie Bear. She *will* be so surprised!"

So off went Bumpy, with a jingle-jingle-jing. Wasn't it nice of Noddy to think of such a treat for him?

THE BUMPY DOG TRIES TO HELP

One morning Noddy went out to his little garage to get his car. " We're going to be busy, car ! " he said. And dear me, it certainly looked as if they were ! See how the little garage is piled with parcels and baskets.

" Sally Skittle is having a sale of work today, to raise money," said Noddy, beginning to polish his car . . . .

" We're going to buy a nice present for Mr. Plod's birthday ! Hallo—who's this ? Oh, it's you, Bumpy Dog ! "

Bumpy came bounding in and upset a pile of parcels. Then he jumped at Noddy joyfully. and knocked him over.

" Oh don't ! " said Noddy. " Why did you have to come on my busy morning ! I've got to pile all these things into my car ! "

THE BUMPY DOG TRIES TO HELP

Soon everything was in—but what a pity, the car wouldn't start ! " *Now* what am I to do ? " said Noddy.

" These things *must* be taken to Sally Skittle's today ! Bumpy—you'll have to help ! " Bumpy was pleased . . . .

He took hold of a basket handle at once and danced round with it proudly. " Be CAREFUL ! " said Noddy. Out spilt the things in the basket—a tin, a bottle, a box—Noddy was very cross. " Wuffy-wuff ! " said Bumpy.

He took hold of a parcel by the string. " That's right," said Noddy. " Take it to Sally Skittle's, Bumpy."

Bumpy was pleased. He threw the parcel up into the air—but alas, he didn't catch it ! Bump—bump . . . .

THE BUMPY DOG TRIES TO HELP

There it was on the ground—and now Noddy could see what was inside it—eggs! Oh dear, look at the mess!

" Wuffy-wuff ! " said Bumpy, and licked it all up. Then he ran to tell Noddy he was sorry —and over went Noddy again !

" Go away," said Noddy. " You're no help at all. Oh, I *wish* my car would start ! Ah—what about that little cart ? "

"It belongs to Bruiny Bear. Bumpy—if I put the things into it, will you pretend to be a horse and pull it ? "

" Wuffy-wuff ! " said Bumpy, in delight. So he helped Noddy to put everything neatly into the cart . . . .

And then Noddy made some reins out of an old rope, and tied Bumpy to the little four-wheeled cart. . . .

THE BUMPY DOG TRIES TO HELP

And away he trotted to Sally Skittle's. Doesn't he look important? Aha—it was fun to be a little horse!

"Neigh-ay-ay! Neigh-ay-ay!" said Bumpy, trotting down the road. He saw Mr. Plod and ran by him, neighing.

Mr. Plod was most surprised. "A dog that neighs like a horse!" he said. "What next? Now then—mind my foot!"

The little cart bumped over the policeman's big boot, and poor Mr. Plod hopped about on one foot, groaning.

Sally Skittle was very pleased to see Bumpy. She took all the things out of the little cart . . . .

And gave Bumpy a nice big biscuit. "Go back and get some more things," she said. So off went Bumpy at top speed . . . .

THE BUMPY DOG TRIES TO HELP

But when he went round a corner on the wrong side, he ran right into Mr. Monkey on his bicycle . . . .

And knocked him off into the road. " I'll tell Mr. Plod of you, you bad dog ! " shouted Mr. Monkey . . . .

And then up came Mr. Plod, frowning. Bumpy fled away back to Noddy's. " Mr. Plod's after you ! " called Monkey.

Bumpy took another load of things to Sally Skittle's, but he went so fast that the little cart fell over . . . .

And everything tumbled into the road. Poor Bumpy ! But who is this coming to help him ? Little Tessie Bear !

" Hallo, Bumpy Dog," she said. " Are you helping Noddy ? Be careful of Mr. Plod—he's very angry with you ! "

THE BUMPY DOG TRIES TO HELP

Well, at last everything was delivered to Sally Skittle's, ready for the sale. What a lot of people were there! Noddy came in his car. He had put it right at last. The sale began—and Sally Skittle took a lot of money.

And then Noddy and Bumpy went off together in the car to buy Mr. Plod's birthday present . . . .

"Look—it's a grand new walking-stick! Hold it, Bumpy, while you sit in the car," said Noddy. "We'll give it to him . . ."

And dear me—how *pleased* Mr. Plod is! "What a beauty!" he said. "And what a fine stick to spank naughty dogs . . . ."

Oh dear—poor Bumpy didn't like that! Away he ran at once. But never mind—he's being asked to the birthday party!

"LET me see now," said Big-Ears, "I've quite a tea-party today. Noddy is coming—and Mr. Plod—and Mr. and Mrs. Noah. I must certainly go down into the town and buy a lot of cakes."

So away he went on his bicycle, a basket tied tightly on behind. He bought a large chocolate cake, some iced buns, a jam sandwich and a new currant loaf. He put them all into his basket and set off home again.

Just as he bicycled round the big old oak tree, a little wind came blowing at him and took off his hat.

"Bother!" said Big-Ears, "that *would* happen when I'm in a hurry!" He got off his bicycle and went to look for his hat—but it had quite disappeared! He was very cross because he had to ride home without it.

Now Noddy was bringing Mr. and Mrs. Noah in his car that afternoon, to have tea with Big-Ears. He drove carefully up the path through the wood, and soon came to the old oak tree.

And *just* as he came there, a little wind blew all round him—and away went his hat—and Mr. and Mrs. Noah's hats, too !

" Stop, stop, Noddy—our hats have blown away ! " they cried and Noddy stopped. " Mine's blown away too, " he said. " I'll go and get them all."

But he couldn't find them ! What a strange thing ! " They're quite gone ! " he called to Mr. and Mrs. Noah, and went back to the car, looking puzzled.

" How peculiar ! " said Mr. Noah. " My head feels quite cold without my hat. "

" Well, we mustn't be late for tea, " said Mrs. Noah. " Drive on, Noddy, and we must look for the hats on our way back. "

So they went on their way to Big-Ears' toadstool house, and he was most surprised to see them all without hats. " Good gracious ! " he said, " did *yours* blow off too ? Mine disappeared as well! "

" Ting-a-ling-a-ling ! " That was Mr. Plod coming along on his bicycle—and how cross he looked !

" I'm sorry not to have on my helmet, " he said, putting his bicycle beside the fence. " But it blew off beside that old oak tree. Whooosh ! Just like that ! What's the wind doing, I'd like to know—hiding there like that, and blowing out all of a sudden ? "

" That's what it did to us too! " said Big-Ears, astonished. " It's taken *all* our hats ! "

" You'll have to lock the wind up in prison, Mr. Plod, " said Noddy, and that made everyone laugh.

" The strange thing is—I thought I heard a little giggle just as my helmet blew off, " said Mr. Plod, frowning. " But I couldn't *see* anyone—and yet I've never heard the wind *giggle* before. I've heard it puff and whoosh and howl and bellow—but I really can't say that I've heard it giggle. "

" Well, Noddy must look hard for all our hats this evening," said Big-Ears. " After all, his has a bell on, and if the wind is *still* blowing by the old oak tree, the bell will ring when the wind blows his hat. "

" Let's have tea, " said Mr. Plod, looking at the chocolate cake in delight. " My word, Big-Ears—what a cake ! And is that currant bread and butter ? I do love that ! "

" I know. That's why I bought it," said Big-Ears and Mr. Plod beamed at him. He looked so cheerful and kind that

Noddy thought he would sit next to him, and he didn't often want to do that!

It was a lovely tea-party and everyone was sorry when it was time to say goodbye. "Noddy, you let Mr. Noah take Mrs. Noah home in your car, and then he can put it into your garage," said Big-Ears. "And you go with Mr. Plod on his bicycle to look for our hats. I don't expect Mr. Plod wants to appear in the town without his helmet. He looks rather peculiar."

So Mr. Noah drove off carefully in Noddy's car, with Mrs. Noah beside him, and Noddy got on the back of Mr. Plod's bicycle. They stopped at the old oak tree.

They hunted for the four hats and one helmet. But not one was to be seen, though they looked under every bush, and up the trees. It was very strange not to find even one.

Noddy was upset about his hat. "I do *miss* hearing my little bell go jingle-jing," he said. "What *are* we going to do, Mr. Plod?"

"I'll have to offer a reward for the hats, I suppose," said

Mr. Plod, gloomily. " Someone's sure to find them—I expect they've blown a long way away. I'll put up the notice tonight."

So when they came to the police-station Noddy watched while Mr. Plod wrote out a big notice. Noddy helped him to nail it up outside.

> 'Lost. Four hats and one helmet. Five pence reward offered to anyone bringing back a hat, and ten pence for the helmet.'

" There ! " said Mr. Plod. " Now perhaps we'll get them back ! Goodbye, Noddy. Thank you for your help."

Well, will you believe it, the very next morning a small goblin called at the police-station with a sack—and in the sack were Mr. and Mrs. Noah's hats, Noddy's hat, and Big-Ears'—*and* Mr. Plod's helmet. He put it on at once.

" Aha ! That's better. Now I feel myself," he said. " Where did you find these, goblin ? "

" Oh—all over the place ! " said the goblin. " The wind must have blown them away ! "

" Well, I know *that* ! " said Mr. Plod. " Here is the reward. Five pence for each of the hats—that's twenty pence—and ten pence for my helmet."

" I wore your helmet for a little while," said the goblin,

and gave a little giggle. "I did feel grand!"

"What! You dared to wear my helmet!" cried Mr. Plod. "I never heard of such. . . ."

But the goblin ran off, with another wicked little giggle. Then up came Noddy, his hair blowing in the wind. He looked funny without his hat. He saw Mr. Plod's helmet at once.

"Oh—you've got your helmet back!" he cried. "Is my hat back too? Who found them?"

"Here's your hat—a little Giggle Goblin brought them back," said Mr. Plod. "I paid him thirty pence reward."

"But Mr. Plod—my *bell* isn't on top," said Noddy, in alarm. "Oh dear! I MUST have my bell. That goblin must have cut it off to keep for himself. Where does he live?"

"Well, the Giggle Goblins live in a cave under a big hollow tree in the Dark Wood," said Mr. Plod, "and. . . ."

But Noddy didn't stop to hear any more! He was off in his car, determined to get back his bell.

How DARE that goblin keep it for himself!

He came to the Dark Wood and made his way to the big hollow tree. Ah—there it was. He hopped out of his car, and ran to it. He climbed into the big hole at the bottom of the trunk and slid down to the caves below.

He listened for the goblins. There wasn't a sound ! " They must have gone to do their shopping, because it's market day," thought Noddy, and he peeped into one little cave.

He couldn't see his bell there, so he went to the next cave and the next. And THEN he saw his bell ! It was on a little shelf, shining brightly. Noddy raced in to get it—and then he saw something else !

" A big pair of bellows ! " he said. " Goodness me—and what's this beside them ? A spell ! Look what's printed on the box. ' SPELLS TO MAKE A LITTLE WIND TO BLOW WASHING OFF LINES OR HATS OFF HEADS ! ' Oh, the *wicked* little goblin ! "

Noddy picked up his bell, the bellows, and the box of spells and ran back to his car. Then he remembered something else and ran back to the cave again. " What about that reward the goblin got ? " he

thought. " He shouldn't have had it. I'll take the money back to Mr. Plod ! "

Yes—there was the money in a little bag in the cupboard. Good, good, good ! Noddy was soon back in his car driving at top speed to Mr. Plod's.

" Mr. Plod ! Mr. Plod ! Where are you ? I've got news ! " cried Noddy. " I've found my bell—and look, here are some spells to make a little wind to blow off hats ! And some bellows to blow them ! That Giggle Goblin must have been hiding up a tree, and he blew the spell at us when we passed by—and away went our hats ! "

" And he picked them up and got the reward ! " said Mr. Plod. " Wait till I get him ! "

" And here's the reward you gave him ! " said Noddy, and gave the surprised Mr. Plod the bag of money. Mr. Plod could hardly believe his eyes.

"Noddy—you've grown some brains at last!" said the big policeman, delighted. "*You* can have the reward now—you deserve it!"

Well, what a wonderful thing! Noddy gave Mr. Plod such a hug that he almost fell over. "I'll give a tea-party now I'm so rich!" he said. "This very day! Will you come, Mr. Plod? Goodbye—I'm off to sew on my bell, and to buy things for my party. Oh, I do feel so happy!"

And away he went and his little car hooted for joy.

"Parp-parp! Parp-parp-PARP!" You really should have heard it!

ONE morning something went wrong with Noddy's car. It made a most peculiar noise underneath, and Noddy couldn't *think* what it was.

" I'll get out and look under the car," he thought, " then I'll soon see what's wrong."

So he got out and crawled under the car. He lay down on his back to see what made the strange noise. " Oh—it's just something come loose," he said. " I can easily tighten that."

Now who should come along at that moment but Tricky Teddy. He was most surprised to see Noddy's car with no Noddy in it—but he soon saw Noddy's feet sticking out from underneath.

" He's putting something right ! " said Tricky Teddy, with a little giggle. " How funny his feet look sticking out there, in their red shoes and blue laces. Shall I tickle them ? "

He was just going to when he suddenly thought of a better idea. " What nice blue laces ! " he said. " I'd like those. I could make a little whip for my top with them. Well—I'll take them out of Noddy's shoes. He won't know who did it, and he'll never be able to get out from under the car quickly enough to catch me ! "

So Tricky pulled out the laces and ran off up the street with them. Noddy felt them being pulled out and he was very

angry indeed—but of course by the time he crept out from under the car, nobody was in sight !

Noddy drove off in his car to Mr. Plod's. Good gracious ! Fancy somebody stealing his laces like that ! What a thing to do ! Mr. Plod should know about that at once.

Mr. Plod was surprised. " Well, well—now *who* would want those old laces of yours ? " he said. " All right, Noddy, I'll look out for them in somebody else's boots ! "

But, of course, Mr. Plod didn't see them in anyone else's boots though he gazed at everyone's feet as they walked along, and made them feel quite uncomfortable.

"Haven't you ever seen my feet before, Mr. Plod ?" said Mr. Monkey, rudely.

And then Mr. Plod suddenly saw Tricky Bear spinning his top most beautifully, watched by Gilbert Golly, Katie Kangaroo, Sue Skittle and Willie Wobbly-Boy.

"See that ?" said Tricky Teddy, proudly. "My top has been spinning for five minutes without stopping. It's all because of my new whip—it's a really fine one."

The others looked at the whip that whipped the top so well. "I never saw a whip with a blue cord before," said Gilbert Golly. "Where did you get it, Tricky ? I'd like to buy one."

"Oh, I'll sell you one. I've got two," said Tricky, and he took one of Noddy's shoe-laces out of his pocket.

"It's only a penny. Have you got a penny, Gilbert ?"

"No," said Gilbert. But Willie Wobbly-Boy had. He held it out to Tricky.

"*I'll* buy it," he said. "I've

got a new top that simply *won't* spin. A whip made with a fine blue cord like that will soon get it going! Look, your top's wobbling, Tricky. Whip it quickly!"

Tricky whipped it, and it spun well again. He was *just* giving the other blue lace to Willie when Mr. Plod came up.

"Tricky, I'd like to see that whip," he said in such a stern voice that everyone trembled, and Katie Kangaroo gave a huge leap right over Mr. Plod's head, and vanished round the corner.

Tricky gave Mr. Plod his whip with a very shaky paw. "HA!" said Mr. Plod. "Where did you get this blue cord for the whip, Tricky?"

"I f-f-f-found it," said Tricky. "It's a very fine whip, Mr. Plod. Please give it back to me."

"A fine whip, did you say?" said Mr. Plod, and cracked it in the air. "Ah yes—very fine indeed. Fine for whipping naughty bears, Tricky—bears that steal shoe laces from other people's shoes. Now then—feel how fine it is!"

And dear me, he gave Tricky Bear *such* a whipping with his boot-lace whip ! All the others fled away at once, and poor Tricky squealed loudly.

" There—I've shown you what a fine whip it is," said Mr. Plod. " Now take the whip and this other shoe-lace to Noddy —do you hear—and tell him you're sorry. You'll be lucky if *he* doesn't try the whip on you too ! "

So there goes Tricky Teddy, tears trickling down his furry nose. He's not only going to say he's sorry, but he's going to give Noddy his lovely top too.

So I don't suppose that Noddy will whip him—he'll be *so* pleased to have his shoe-laces back again, and to be able to keep his shoes on properly.

And I feel quite sure that he won't use them to spin the top !